MW01488000

The Nuts and Bolts of Autism
of Autism
2nd Edition

Dr. Linda Barboa

Jan Luck

Dedicated to the memory of Mike Barboa

Published by KIP Educational Materials
ISBN-13: 978-1542958844
ISBN-10: 1542958849

WHAT IS AUTISM?

Autism is a complex disorder. As we go through our everyday lives, our brains continually collect information about the world around us through our senses (including vision, hearing, smell, touch and taste). In autism, the senses may be over or under processing the incoming stimuli. People with autism are not able to make sense of the incoming sensory information. The issues may vary throughout a person's lifetime, or even day to day.

WHAT ARE THE MAIN PROBLEMS ASSOCIATED WITH AUTISM?

The core features of autism include:
- disorders in communication
- sensory issues
- difficulty in social interactions
- unusual behaviors.

WHAT IS A SPECTRUM DISORDER?

You will hear autism referred to as a "spectrum disorder". This means that the person's abilities and behaviors fall along a very wide range from high functioning to low functioning. The outward signs vary greatly from person to person. Autism spectrum disorder is often abbreviated ASD.

HOW COMMON IS AUTISM?

The Center for Disease Control and Prevention (CDC)[i] estimates that one in 68 children has autism, with the rate being one in every 42 boys. The identified rate is five times higher in boys than girls. It is one of the fastest growing developmental disabilities in the United States. Autism affects people of all races, nationalities and social classes.

As of this printing, there are approximately 3.5 million Americans living with autism.

HOW IS AUTISM DIAGNOSED?

There is no medical test for autism. Specially trained physicians, neurologists, and psychologists diagnose it through behavioral observations and analysis.

WHAT DOES AUTISM LOOK LIKE?

Although the characteristics vary widely from person to person there is a set of "red flags" that are common in this group of people. They include, among other things:

- Difficulty in regulating emotions
- Difficulty in interacting with others
- Delayed babbling or speech delay
- Inability to understand body language
- Odd, unusual or repetitive behaviors
- May have lost skills previously acquired
- Over-sensitivity or under-sensitivity to things they see, hear, smell, taste, or feel. [ii]

WHAT CAUSES AUTISM?

There are many theories as to the cause of autism and why it is increasing at such a fast rate. It is suspected that there may be a genetic factor and an environmental factor, although no cause has been proven. The important thing to know is that it is not caused by the parents behavior. Theories about autism being caused by emotionally cold parents have been long disproven. You may see claims made on almost a daily basis of causes and links to autism, but at this point there is not a known cause- just many theories.

DOES AUTISM RUN IN FAMILIES?

There does seem to be an indication that it is more prevalent in some families. Even though autism runs in some families, we can't say it is totally "inherited".[iii]

WHAT ARE SPLINTER SKILLS?

A characteristic of many people on the spectrum is the uneven pattern of development of their skills and abilities. They may have certain skills that are far more advanced than their other abilities. Those higher skills are known as splinter skills.

HOW ARE SOCIAL SKILLS AFFECTED?

Appropriate social interactions are important for a happy and productive life. Forging friendships and having good relationships with others is dependent on successful social interactions. People on the autism spectrum may exhibit some or all of these social difficulties:

- Difficulty with eye contact
- Inability to interpret facial expression or other gestures
- Poor social or emotional connections
- Little or no interest in others
- Lack the
- ability to see things from another's point of view
- Lack of understanding humor
- Very literal thinking
- Extreme attachments to a toy or other object
- May play with toys in unusual or unexpected ways
- May be afraid of things they need not fear and not fear things that most people are afraid of
- May shun or crave physical contact with others
- Needs predictability and routine- change is difficult
- May do unusual actions repeatedly

HOW ARE COMMUNICATION SKILLS AFFECTED?

Communication is our most basic connection to others in our world. When the ability to communicate effectively is missing, it interferes with a full and happy life. Communication skills may be affected in many ways including:

- Lack of a social "filter"- they say what they think although the comment may be inappropriate or hurtful
- May be delayed in language development
- May remain basically nonverbal
- May repeat words, phrases or entire paragraphs that they have heard before
- May speak in a flat tone of voice
- May have difficulty constructing sentences
- May use some basic sign language or an electronic communication device

HOW IS PHYSICAL CONTACT AFFECTED?

Many people with autism avoid physical contact with others. The touch from another person may actually be painful as their sense of touch is overly developed. There are others who are perfectly fine with having another touch them, especially if they are the one to initiate the physical contact. Often a stronger, firm touch is more accepted by him than a light, feathery touch, which may even feel painful.

HOW ARE THE SENSES INVOLVED?

Distorted sensory perception is a major part of autism. The way a person with autism perceives the world around him is different from the way that others get that information from the environment. Any one or more of the senses can be affected. The person may perceive the incoming stimuli as being too much or too little. This may vary from day to day. A small amount of anything in the environment may be overwhelming, or a large amount may seem like not enough. The person may constantly try to avoid or seek things to affect any of the senses.

The senses involved may include:

- Vision: Person may seek or avoid light or visual movement.
- Hearing: It may be impossible to distinguish the voice of someone speaking from the background noises. Speech and background noise may all melt together.
- Taste: The person ingesting a harmful substance or appearing to be very picky.
- Smell: The person may be drawn to noxious odors or repulsed by pleasant smells.
- Feeling and touch: Things as soft as clothing, or even air may be extremely uncomfortable to him.
- Vestibular: The person may appear clumsy.
- Proprioception: He may bump into things or fall.
- Interoception: He may not correctly interpret internal bodily signals such as hunger, pain, tiredness, nausea, or emotions.

HOW ARE BEHAVIORS AFFECTED?

As children learn to cope with overwhelming situations they may develop coping skills that are positive or skills which are negative. Behavior is an attempt to communicate his needs, his sensory overloads and his frustrations. Behaviors that may occur include:

- Withdrawal
- Aggression
- Self-stimulation such as rocking, jumping, flapping the hands, humming or chanting
- Meltdowns
- Unusual pattern of interests, such as high interest in one topic, like dinosaurs, vacuums, or the solar system

IS A MELTDOWN JUST A TEMPER TANTRUM?

A meltdown is different from a tantrum. Temper tantrums are thrown by a child who wants something such as a toy, or wants to avoid something, such as chores. When he gets what he wants, the tantrum ends. He relies on having an audience, and normally will not continue the tantrum otherwise. A meltdown, on the other hand, is a very intense reaction to being overwhelmed or overstressed. This does not end by reaching a goal, but more likely ends by fatigue setting in. A meltdown is not dependent on having an audience. The person may truly need help to regain control.

WHAT MEDICAL CONDITIONS ARE ASSOCIATED WITH AUTISM?

There seems to be a high tendency for children with autism to have other medical problems, including but not limited to:

- Gastrointestinal disorders
- Seizures
- Sleep dysfunction
- Sensory processing disorders
- Hyperactivity
- Attention deficit disorder
- Pica (tendency to eat non-edible objects)

HOW IS AUTISM TREATED?

There are many options available. Some people prefer to use bio-medical procedures. Others believe that behavioral approaches work best. Still others use a combination of treatments. Educational interventions include therapies from an occupational therapist to help with sensory issues and a speech-language pathologist to support the communication needs. Behavioral services can be provided by specially trained Board Certified Behavior Analysts or their assistants. Behavioral therapists can also provide treatments. All of the professionals discussed here can provide services to support the child's teacher. These treatments help the child develop higher communication skills and social interactions, thus enabling better learning.

WHAT IS ASPERGER'S SYNDROME?

Asperger's Syndrome is one form of autism, on the higher functioning end of the autism spectrum. People with Asperger's usually have difficulties with social situations but not with language development. They are often very literal thinkers and struggle to understand humor, figures of speech, sarcasm and words with multiple meanings. They may be rigid in their schedules. People with Asperger's usually function well in daily life and in society even though they struggle with social expectations and understandings.

WHAT IS PERVASIVE DEVELOPMENTAL DISORDER (PDD-NOS)?

Sometimes this term is used interchangeably with the word "autism". Other times it refers to a person who has some, but not all of the symptoms of classic autism. The defining features of PDD-NOS are significant challenges in social and language development.

DO PEOPLE EVER PROGRESS TO THE POINT THAT THEY MOVE OFF THE SPECTRUM?

Growing evidence suggests that a small number of people actually progress in the core areas that define autism, to actually move off the autism spectrum. Studies show that early identification and intervention significantly improves outcomes.

ARE ALL PEOPLE WITH AUTISM GENIUSES?

The Center for Autism and Related Disorders estimates that less than 5% of people with autism score cognitively at the genius level.[iv] The phenomena of splinter skills, discussed earlier, may give the impression of a higher level of functioning than what it actually is. Just as people who do not have autism exhibit skills all along the range of intellectual abilities, the same applies to those with autism. Intellectual skills may range from intellectually challenged to gifted.

WHAT SHOULD I DO IF I SUSPECT MY CHILD HAS AUTISM?

A good place to start is by talking to your pediatrician.
Make this contact as soon as possible. Your doctor can give you the information needed to contact services for diagnosis and treatment. A helpful book to read at that point is *Stars in Her Eyes; Navigating the Maze of Childhood Autism* by Barboa and Obrey (2014). This book will lead you by the hand through the diagnosis process and into intervention decisions. Do not fear the diagnosis, as that can be the key to unlock many doors, such as educational services and financial assistance. It is also helpful to talk to others who have children on the spectrum, as they can lead you to resources and services in your area.

IF I SEE A CHILD HAVING A MELTDOWN, HOW CAN I HELP?

Remember that the parent has been through this before and knows the child best. While it is acceptable to calmly ask the parent if there is anything you can do to help, please respect the parent's decision. If she tells you that she has the situation in control, move on and allow the parent to work through the meltdown. Do not make judgmental comments or give disapproving looks. If the meltdown is occurring in a grocery store, for example, and the parent has a grocery cart of food she is trying to purchase, you could offer to help her checkout while she maintains the situation with the child.

CAN PEOPLE WITH AUTISM BECOME PRODUCTIVE MEMBERS OF SOCIETY?

High functioning people on the spectrum are likely to be very successful in college and excel in the fields of science and medicine. Traits commonly noted in people with autism, such as a strong need for structure and intense focus on interests, can be an assets in the work force in many different fields. Adaptations and modifications are often needed, along with special training for both the individual and the employer. Although they may need extensive assistance, most people on the autism spectrum can become contributing members of society.

WHAT DO PEOPLE WITH AUTISM NEED WHEN THEY BECOME ADULTS?

Adults with autism often have some special needs. Each person's needs will differ, but this is a list of needs that many have in common:

- Vocational training based on the person's strengths and interests
- Job opportunities where the employer and co-workers have been trained to understand the challenges of autism
- Group homes, supervised apartments, or other alternate living arrangements
- Recreational and social opportunities where they can feel accepted and not judged

Autism involves continuous, lifelong progress in all areas, including social awareness, learning new skills and finding new enjoyable experiences.ᵛ What do adults with autism need to be successful as adults? They need compassionate, continuous support in areas that others take for granted. They need understanding from the community as they try hard to lead fulfilling lives.

WHAT MORE CAN I DO TO HELP?

Stars for Autism is a non-profit organization. Its mission is to network, collaborate, promote and support efforts, training, awareness, respect, and service for individuals and families with autism. Stars for Autism provides education and literature to teach people about autism.

Muse Watson
(AKA Mike Franks, NCIS)

Mr. Muse Watson is the Honorary Chairman of this organization. He is passionate about the need for people to learn about autism and regularly advocates for this cause.

If you would like to support this effort, please visit our website for more information.

www.Stars4autism.org

WHAT DO THESE TERMS AND ACRONYMS MEAN?

As you navigate the maze of autism, you will find yourself dealing with some terms and acronyms which may be unfamiliar to you. This guide will give you a brief explanation of those which are among the most commonly used.

AACs: Augmentative and alternative communication devices. Electronic devices used to speak for the mostly non-verbal person.

ABA: Applied Behavior Analysis. A structured program that many parents feel is highly successful. Used by trained professionals.

ADD: Attention Deficit Disorder.

ADHD: Hyperactivity added to ADD.

Alerting stimulants: Things in the environment which make the child more alert or more awake.

Aromatherapy: Some smells may be invigorating while others may be soothing to the child.

Articulation: The way we pronounce our words.

ASD: Autism Spectrum Disorder.

Asperger's Syndrome: A form of autism which is characterized by social awkwardness.

Aspie: An affectionate term for a person with Asperger's.

Attachment: A person with autism may become highly attached to a certain object.

Auditory: The sense of hearing.

Auditory processing: The system by which the brain makes sense of the sounds that we hear.

Auditory sensitivities: Child may be overly or under sensitive to sounds.

AutPlay ® Therapy: Developed by Dr. Robert Grant, this method combines behavioral and developmental techniques.

Avoidance behavior: A learned coping mechanism in which the person with autism withdraws from a situation to escape some stimuli that is aversive to him.

Babbling: Early speech sounds such as, "mama" or "dada" which are normal speech productions for a baby.

Behavioral: Any action that is not purely reflexive.

Biomedical: Treatments that address physical symptoms.

BIP: Behavior Intervention Plan implemented by a school.

Brushing: A therapy technique used to produce a calming, sensory organizing effect.

Calming skills: Persons with autism may need to be taught techniques to calm themselves.

Casein: A protein in dairy that may have an adverse effect on some people.

ChoicesChat© short simple chats you have with a child about choices he has made, and what may be a better choice the next time.[vi] First identified by Barboa and Obrey in 2015.

Co-morbidities: Other diagnoses that occur along with the primary issue.

Coping skills: People learn to cope with unpleasant situations in a variety of ways. Some coping skills are negative and others are positive.

Cycling: Some children will learn a skill, lose the skill, and need to re-learn it, in a cyclical fashion.

Deep pressure: A therapy technique for calming and making sense of incoming sensations.

Discrete Trial Training: A highly structured method of teaching used by highly trained professionals.

DSM: Diagnostic and Statistical Manual of Mental Disorders, used as criteria for diagnosing disorders.

Early Intervention: Identification and treatment that begins in early childhood.

Echolalia: Repetition of a sound, word or phrase that the child has heard another person say.

Expressive Language: The language that the person can actually produce.

Flapping: A sensory stimulating activity in which a child flaps his hands or arms.

Gluten: A protein in some grains which has an adverse effect on some people.

Gustatory: The sense of taste.

Hyperacusis: An abnormal reaction to sound.

Hyperlexia: A splinter skill of being able to decode reading words at a higher level than he can comprehend.

Hypersensitive: Overly sensitive.

Hyposensitive: Too low sensitivity.

IDEA: Individuals with Disabilities Education Act. Federal law guarantees a free and appropriate education for all children.

IEP: Individual Education Plan (or Program). Plan developed by the parent and the school to provide for the child's educational needs.

Incidental learning: Learning that happens informally.

Inclusion: When special education services are brought into the regular classroom to individualize instruction.

Joint attention: Communication between two people.

Learned helplessness: When we provide too much help for a child rather than expecting him to do things for himself, he will take longer to learn that skill.

Mainstreaming: The process of integrating your child into a typical classroom.

Melatonin: A plant product sold as a supplement.

Meltdowns: Overstimulation which results in the child being overwhelmed and losing control.

Occupational therapy: Can help balance out sensory perceptions.

Olfactory: Sense of smell.

Parental rights: In the educational system these are designated by law.

PECS®: Picture Exchange Communication System. Technique used by specially trained professions, using small pictures to communicate.

Perseveration: Repetition of a movement or sound.

PDD: Pervasive Developmental Disorder. May be used interchangeably with the word "autism" or may refer to a child who has some of the characteristics, but not all.

Pica: Desire to eat non-edible objects such as dirt.

Pragmatics: The social aspect of speech, such as greetings and conversational skills.

Predictability: People with autism usually have a deep need to know the schedule.

PrepChat©: Developed by Barboa and Obrey, this is a simplified chat that you have with the child to discuss an upcoming event and prepare him for what he will encounter.

Proprioception: The sensory system that informs your child of the position of his body in relation to the space around him.

QR codes©: Patches registered online which can be sewn into clothing to be scanned to reveal the child's important identifying information. Developed by "If I Need Help", a non-profit organization.

Quiet rooms: Rooms in a public place such as a theater or church where parents or teachers can calm children who are getting overwhelmed.

Receptive language: The vocabulary that a person can understand as opposed to what he produces.

Reinforcers: Rewards given for behaviors or tasks completed.

Respite: Help given by another to take care of the person who has special needs to give the parent or guardian a break.

Rett's Disorder: A genetic disorder which results in behaviors of autism.

Rituals: Routines or activities that the person seems compelled to perform, such as flicking the light on and off multiple times.

Scaffolding: Refers to the assistance given to a child in learning to complete a task. Like a painter standing on a scaffold to reach higher than he could otherwise, teaching techniques help the child achieve higher levels of learning.

Scripting: People repeating segments of conversations or television shows they have heard.

Self-injurious behaviors: Behaviors by a person to willfully inflict harm on himself.

Self-stimulation: When a person creates stimuli or sensory input for himself, such as rocking, flapping, or spinning.

Sensory input: The stimulation received through the environment.

Sensory integration: Processing information received from the body and the environment.

Social referencing: When a child looks to others for approval or acknowledgement.

Splinter skills: Talents that are far above the rest of the person's abilities.

Stimming/ self-stim: See "self-stimulation."

Stimuli/ stimulus: Anything that creates a reaction in the person.

Tactile: The sense of touch.

Tactile defensiveness: Not wanting to be touched.

Task analysis: Breaking down a job into its smaller steps.

Transitioning: Changing from one activity to the next. This is often a special challenge for children on the spectrum.

Vestibular activities: Jumping, rocking, balancing, swinging, etc.

Weighted vests: A calming strategy used under the direction of an occupational therapist.

ABOUT THE AUTHORS

Dr. Linda Barboa   Jan Luck

Dr. Linda Barboa is an experienced speech-language pathologist, with a background as a special education director, director of a center for autism, and university professor. She has worked as an educator in the United States and Europe. Dr. Barboa currently resides in Battlefield, Missouri near her son, Christopher, and his family. She is the founder of Stars for Autism, and is the recipient of the prestigious Jefferson Award for Public Service.

Jan Luck holds a degree in speech pathology and audiology. In her career she worked for the State of Arkansas serving clients of all ages with special needs and in public schools. Mrs. Luck has developed and presented continuing education seminars on the topic of autism for teachers, therapists, and parents. She currently resides in Nixa, Missouri, where she is the president of Stars for Autism, Inc.

Helpful Books About Autism by These Authors:

Stars in Her Eyes; Navigating the Maze of Childhood Autism, by Dr. Linda Barboa and Elizabeth Obrey

Steps: Forming a Disability Ministry, by Shelli Allen and Dr. Linda Barboa

Tic Toc Autism Clock; A Guide to Your 24/7 Plan, by Elizabeth Obrey and Dr. Linda Barboa

It's No Biggie; Autism in the Early Childhood Classroom, by Dr. Linda Barboa and Mary Datema

Children's Books About Autism by These Authors:

Albert is My Friend; Helping Children Understand Autism (also available in Spanish, German, and Dutch).

Albert Thinks About His Future

Albert Goes to School

Albert Goes to Church

Albert Goes to Camp

Albert Builds a Friend Ship

Oodles and Skoodles of Friends

[i] http://www.cdc.gov/ncbddd/autism/data.html Aug 12, 2015.

[ii] Barboa, L. and Obrey, E. *Stars in Her Eyes; Navigating the Maze of Childhood Autism,* (Mustang, Oklahoma: Tate Publishing 2014)

[iii] https://www.autismspeaks.org/blog/2012/11/30/autism-predisposition-among-children-adult-siblings

[iv] http://www.centerforautism.com/home.aspx, March 1, 2016

[v] Becker, L. *Autism and the World According to Matt,* (Mustang, Oklahoma: Tate Publishing 2015)

[vi] Obrey, E., and Barboa, L. *Tic Toc Autism Clock,* (Nashville, Tennessee: Goldminds Publishing 2015)

Made in the USA
Columbia, SC
14 March 2019